LET'S FIND OUT! PLANTS

WHERE PLANTS GROW

REBECCA KRAFT RECTOR

Britannica Educational Publishing
IN ASSOCIATION WITH
ROSEN
EDUCATIONAL SERVICES

Published in 2019 by Britannica Educational Publishing (a trademark of Encyclopædia Britannica, Inc.) in association with The Rosen Publishing Group, Inc.
29 East 21st Street, New York, NY 10010

Distributed exclusively by Rosen Publishing.
To see additional Britannica Educational Publishing titles, go to rosenpublishing.com.

First Edition

Britannica Educational Publishing
J.E. Luebering: Executive Director, Core Editorial
Mary Rose McCudden: Editor, Britannica Student Encyclopedia

Rosen Publishing
Louise Eaton: Editor
Nelson Sá: Art Director
Nicole Russo-Duca: Series Designer/Book Layout
Cindy Reiman: Photography Manager
Ellina Litmanovich: Photo Researcher

Library of Congress Cataloging-in-Publication Data

Names: Rector, Rebecca Kraft, author.
Title: Where plants grow / Rebecca Kraft Rector.
Description: New York : Britannica Educational Publishing, in Association with Rosen Educational Services, 2019. | Series: Let's find out! Plants | Audience: Grades 1–4. | Includes bibliographical references and index.
Identifiers: LCCN 2017044424| ISBN 9781538302057 (library bound) | ISBN 9781538302064 (pbk.) | ISBN 9781538302071 (6 pack)
Subjects: LCSH: Phytogeography—Juvenile literature. | Plant ecology—Juvenile literature. | Plants—Habitat—Juvenile literature.
Classification: LCC QK101 .R345 2019 | DDC 581.7—dc23
LC record available at https://lccn.loc.gov/2017044424

Manufactured in the United States of America

Photo credits: Cover, interior pages background Ricardo Reitmeyer/Shutterstock.com; p. 4 Photos.com/Jupiter Images; p. 5 Neal Herbert/U.S. National Park Service; pp. 6, 8, 23 © Encyclopædia Britannica, Inc.; p. 7 Ongala /Shutterstock.com; p. 9 E.R. Degginger; p. 10 © Lynn Abercrombie; p. 11 © Grant Heilman Photography; p. 12 Ana Flasker/Shutterstock.com; p. 13 Greg Dimijian/Science Source/Getty Images; p. 14 © Eva Lemonenko /Fotolia; p. 15 © Ingmar Holmasen; p. 16 © Jeremy D. Rogers; p. 17 Pi-Lens/Shutterstock.com; p. 18 © pannoneantonio/Fotolia; p. 19 © Earth Observatory/NASA; p. 20 cristalvi/Shutterstock.com; p. 21 © A to Z Botanical Collection/Encyclopædia Britannica, Inc.; p. 22 sanderstock/Fotolia; p. 24 Eugeny Moskvitin/Fotolia; p. 25 Pim Leijen/Fotolia; p. 26 skyf/Fotolia; p. 27 © Lesly/Fotolia; p. 28 Shannon West/Shutterstock.com; p. 29 © Matthias Sebulke.

Contents

Plants Grow Almost Everywhere

Plants are living things that do not move around. They live and grow in one spot. Trees, flowers, and vegetables are examples of plants. Many plants are green, but some are not. Most plants need sun, air, and water to survive. Parasitic plants, however, get food and water from another plant.

Vocabulary

Parasitic describes a living thing that depends on another living thing for existence or support without offering anything in return.

Lilies grow in temperate areas of the Northern Hemisphere.

Many different living things can live in one habitat.

Plants cannot move from place to place, but they can grow in almost any habitat. A habitat is an environment where something lives. There are plant habitats both on land and in the water. The habitats can be hot, warm, or cold. On land, they can also be wet or dry, like a swamp or a desert. Plants with similar needs grow in the same habitats. Most plants grow in soil. Some plants grow in water and some even grow under water. A kind of plant called an epiphyte grows on other plants or rocks.

Forests

A forest is a place where many trees grow. Forests grow in almost every part of the world. The only places bare of forests are deserts, some prairies and mountaintops, and the North and South poles. Some thick forests grow in warm, wet areas. These are called tropical rainforests. Forests in cold areas just south of the North Pole are called taiga.

Most forest trees are called either hardwoods or softwoods. The two kinds of trees usually do not grow in the same forest. Hardwood forests grow where the weather is mild or

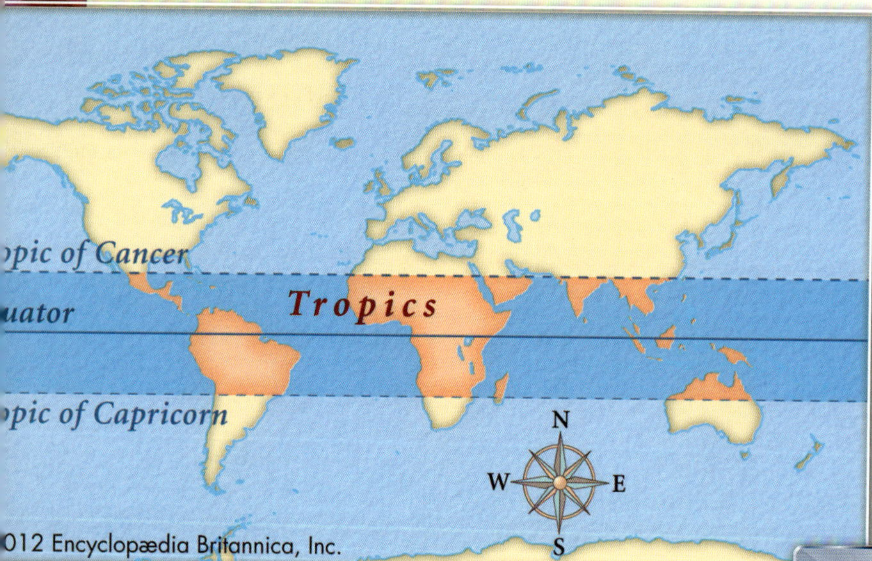

The plants that grow in the tropics, where it is very warm, are different than those that grow in colder areas.

Think About It

Why do you think hardwoods and softwoods usually do not grow in the same forest?

Most hardwood trees have leaves that change colors in the autumn.

hot. Hardwoods grow fruits. They also have wide leaves.

Softwood forests grow where the weather is cool. Softwood trees have cones and needles. These trees are often called evergreens. Other forest plants include bushes and vines. Wildflowers and ferns also grow in forests.

Tropical Rainforests

Different kinds of plants grow at different levels of a tropical rainforest.

Tropical rainforests exist in hot, wet areas of the world. It rains frequently in tropical rainforests.

Rainforests have different layers made up of plants of different heights. Tall tree branches make up the top layer, called the canopy. Under the canopy is the understory. It is darker there. Finally, there is the floor of the forest. The floor is also dark.

This blooming orchid is an epiphyte that gets nutrients from the air and rain.

Many kinds of plants live in the rainforest. Small trees and shrubs grow in the understory. Epiphytes live on the trees in the canopy and understory layers. They do not touch the ground. They get their nutrients from the air and rain. Many types of orchids are epiphytes.

Compare and Contrast

What is different about plants that live in the understory and plants that live on the forest floor? What is the same?

Parasitic vines, like the strangler fig, also live on the trees. They get their nutrients from the trees. Ferns and fungi live on the forest floor. They do not need much sunlight so they can survive in the dark conditions at that level of the rainforest.

Deserts

Most deserts get fewer than 10 inches (25 centimeters) of rain in a year.

Deserts are dry. In fact, it seldom rains in deserts. Deserts are known for being sandy, but not all deserts are sandy. Mountains and rocks can also exist in deserts.

There are hot deserts and cold deserts. Antarctica, the land around the South Pole, is a cold desert. The Sahara in Africa is a hot desert.

Desert plants and animals have features that help them survive in the dry climate. Some plants are able to grow in the desert because they have very long roots. The roots grow long to find water deep underground.

Tamarisk shrubs are an example of plants with roots that find water underground.

Some plants, like many kinds of cactus, store water. If it rains, grasses, wildflowers, and small shrubs quickly begin to grow. Some seeds sprout right after rain. They quickly bloom and make seeds. When the ground dries up, the plant dies. The new seeds must wait for the next rain before they grow.

Think About It

Why do some plants grow, bloom, and make seeds quickly after a rain?

Cacti, like this prickly pear cactus, can bloom after a rain.

POLAR REGIONS

The polar regions are the areas around the North Pole and the South Pole. The area around the North Pole is called the Arctic, and the area around the South Pole is called Antarctica.

The polar regions are very cold. Polar regions receive little rain, so they are called cold deserts. Many places in the Arctic are always frozen. The flat, low land is called tundra. Snow covers the ground for half the year.

Reindeer eat grass in the snowy Arctic. Many other plants cannot survive in the cold polar regions.

Most of the polar regions have few plants. Plants must be able to live through long, dark winters. However, short grasses and mosses may grow there. Trees only grow in the southern part of the Arctic. There are no trees in Antarctica. The coast of Antarctica has areas without ice, and mosses and liverworts grow there.

Vocabulary

Liverworts are plants that look like flat leaves.

Antarctic hair grass grows on a hill near a colony of penguins.

Grasslands

Large areas of grass are called grasslands. Usually, grasslands are flat. Sometimes there are rolling hills. The grasses may be short or tall. Grasses grow well in wide open spaces.

Temperate grasslands have hot summers and cold winters. The prairies of North America are temperate grasslands. So are the pampas of Argentina, the veld of southern Africa, and the steppes of central Asia.

Most grasslands receive enough rain

Yaks graze in grasslands.

Think About It

Why would trees need more rain to grow than grasses?

for grass. Wildflowers and crops like wheat, oats, and corn may also grow in grasslands. Trees, however, need more rain than grasslands provide.

Tropical grasslands are also often called savannas. They grow where it is hot all year. Savanna grasses are rough and thick. A few trees may be found in the savanna.

Africa's Serengeti Plain is a tropical grassland, or savanna.

Mountains

Mountains are land formations that rise high above the surrounding land. They are formed from rock.

Mountains exist in many areas. There are mountains in deserts and grasslands. There are also mountains in forests and tundra.

Mountains have different habitats at different heights. Forests of fir and pine trees often grow lower on a mountain. Shrubs may be found where there is soil. Wildflowers grow on mountainsides.

Bare rock covers the top of Mount Rainier in the state of Washington.

Compare and Contrast

How are mountain areas similar to grasslands? How are they different?

Plants must be tough to live high in the mountains. It is often windy and dry, and the soil is thin. Also, water runs down from mountaintops, so higher up, there is less water. When water is present, it can wash away loose soil. Some high mountain points have no soil at all. Overall, the growing season is short and cold. Higher up, it becomes too cold for trees to survive. However, mosses and liverworts grow in high mountain areas.

Wildflowers grow in a mountainside meadow.

Oceans and Seashores

The ocean is a large body of saltwater. Most plants grow near the surface of the water, where there is sunlight. Deeper waters are farther away from the light above, so they are darker. There are no green plants in the deep sea.

Most ocean plants are **phytoplankton**. Some phytoplankton are no bigger than a single cell. Seaweed and kelp, some other ocean plants, are plant-like algae. Some kinds

Some plants are adapted to live along rocky seashores, like those of the Cape Peninsula in South Africa.

The swirls of lighter blue are large numbers of phytoplankton growing in the water.

of seaweed float in the ocean. Most seaweeds grow in shallow water near the shore. Seagrass, another kind of ocean plant, also grows in shallow water, often in underwater meadows.

Hardy plants grow where the ocean meets the shore. These plants are strong enough to live among the waves and salty water. Mangrove trees have roots in the water and in the air. They are one of the few trees that can grow in saltwater. Near the water's edge, plants grow on sand dunes and clifftops. These include grasses and sea lavender.

VOCABULARY

Phytoplankton are tiny plants that float near the top of the water.

Lakes and Ponds

Water lilies grow from the muddy bottom of the water. The leaves usually float on the surface.

Lakes are large bodies of water that are surrounded by land. The water moves slowly or not at all. Most lakes are deep and have freshwater. Some have salt water.

Ponds are smaller than lakes and are not as deep. They have freshwater.

Lakes and ponds are home to many plants. These plants must be able to grow in wet conditions. Most plants grow near the surface of the water, where there is more light. Phytoplankton grows in the water of deep lakes.

Some pond plants grow under the water. Water milfoil is one of those plants.

Water lilies and reeds grow in ponds and at the edges of lakes. They have roots in the soil below the water. The rest of the plant rises above the water.

Think About It

Why might the water lily bloom on top of the water instead of under the water? Which area gets more light?

Water milfoil grows under the water surface.

WETLANDS

A wetland is a place where water does not drain well. The soil is usually very wet. Water often covers the ground. Wetlands are found on every continent except Antarctica.

There are three kinds of wetlands. These are marshes, bogs, and swamps. Marshes and swamps are similar. They both have a lot of minerals. Both can have freshwater or salt water. They form along rivers or coasts. Bogs get most of their water from rain. Rainwater contains few minerals, so the soil in bogs does not have a lot of minerals.

Bogs get most of their water from rain. Few plants grow in bogs.

Compare and Contrast

What is different about the three kinds of wetlands? What is the same?

Different plants grow in each type of wetland. Trees grow in swamps, and grasses grow in marshes. Cattails and reeds grow in swamps, while wildflowers grow in marshes. Only a few kinds of plants grow in bogs. Mosses and heaths grow there.

Pond cypress trees grow in the Okefenokee Swamp in Georgia and northern Florida.

Rivers and Streams

A river is a long body of water that flows over the land. Rivers often flow into an ocean. The water of a river is fresh, not salty. Streams are smaller bodies of water that flow into rivers.

Rivers and streams are filled with water plants. Many of these plants have parts that keep them from being washed away in flowing water. Strong roots and stems that bend with the flow of water keep them grounded and flexible.

A stream curves through the countryside.

Foxes drink at a grassy riverbank.

VOCABULARY

A **riverbank** is the ground at the edge of a river.

Stream plants include water lilies and arrowhead plants. Reeds can be found on the edges of streams. Mosses can grow on river rocks.

Many plants grow along a riverbank. The cottonwood tree, one plant that grows along riverbanks, likes sunny, wet areas. Sedges are grass-like plants that also grow along riverbanks. Willow trees have roots that grow deep into the ground. They grow near rivers.

FARMS AND GARDENS

A farm is a place where people grow plants and raise animals for human use. Gardens usually cover a smaller area of land. People may eat the plants of a farm or garden, enjoy their beauty, or sell what they grow.

The plants of a farm or garden may not be native to the area. These plants originally grew somewhere else and then people brought them to the new area. For example, carrots first grew in southern Europe,

Cows need fields of healthy grass to graze on.

Trees, shrubs, and grasses grow in this Japanese garden.

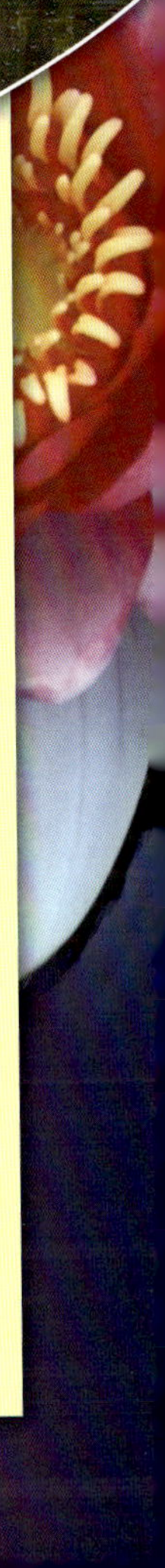

VOCABULARY

Native describes something that lives or grows naturally in a certain place.

and potatoes are native to South America. People still bring plants to new areas.

Generally, any plant can grow in a farm or garden if the grower can create the right conditions. Different plants require different temperatures and amounts of light. For example, flower growers provide shade for pansies. They make sure petunias grow in sun. Pumpkins and tomatoes do not like cold. They must be protected from frost. Herbs like lavender are grown in hot and dry areas.

Homes, Offices, and Greenhouses

Plants can be grown inside homes and offices. There, it is usually warm and dry, and insects cannot access plants easily. But people must take care of indoor plants by putting them in pots with soil and fertilizer and by watering them.

Some people grow plants in greenhouses. Greenhouses are like gardens but indoors. They are buildings with glass walls and a glass ceiling. The glass lets the light in and protects the plants from harsh weather. Inside, the temperature and moisture can be controlled.

Potted plants grow on a sunny windowsill.

Think About It

Is the indoors a better habitat for plants than outdoors? Why or why not?

Greenhouses are bright and can hold many plants.

Tropical plants grow well indoors. Philodendrons and dumb canes are popular. Cacti also grow well. Geraniums grow and bloom in sunny windows. Rubber trees and palms grow well in big pots. Small orange trees can also grow well.

Plants are all around in nature and even in some indoor settings. If an environment can fulfill their needs, they will grow and reproduce.

Enormous lily pads and other tropical plants grow in this greenhouse in Germany.

Glossary

drain To empty a liquid out of an area by spreading out or sinking down.

environment A place with a set of features.

epiphyte A plant that grows on trees but does not rely on the tree for nourishment.

freshwater Water that is not salty.

fungi Living things that are similar to plants but that do not have roots, stems, or leaves. Mushrooms are fungi.

habitat The place where a plant or animal lives or grows.

hardy Strong; able to survive unfavorable conditions.

heath A kind of shrub that grows in open areas with wet soil.

land formation Land that is shaped in a specific way.

minerals Substances that do not come from an animal or a plant; plants and animals need them to live.

moss Small, seedless plant that often grows in moist, shady places.

nutrients Substances that nourish a living being's body.

provide To offer.

region A broad area of land.

salt water Water from the sea.

shallow Not deep at all.

shrub A short plant with several woody stems that produces leaves and sometimes fruit.

soil Dirt, especially used for growing plants.

surface An outside part or layer of something.

temperate A kind of climate that is mild, without very hot or cold temperatures.

tropical A kind of climate found in places near the equator, where the weather is very warm.

wildflower The flower of a wild plant or the plant that bears it.

For More Information

Books

Gregory, Cam. *Where Do Tall Trees Grow?* Beaverton, OR: Three Crows Media, 2013.

Hawley, Ella. *Exploring Ecosystems*. New York, NY: PowerKids Press, 2013.

Hibbert, Clare. *Seaside Plants and Animals*. London, UK: Franklin Watts, 2015.

MacAulay, Kelley. *How Do Plants Survive?* St. Catharines, ON: Crabtree Publishing, 2014.

Riley, Peter D. *Habitats*. London, UK: Franklin Watts, 2016.

Roumanis, Alexis. *Deserts*. New York, NY: AV2, 2016.

Roumanis, Alexis. *Rainforests*. New York, NY: AV2, 2016.

Spilsbury, Louise. *What Are Habitats & Biomes?* New York, NY: Britannica Educational Publishing, 2014.

Websites

BBC
http://www.bbc.co.uk/nature/habitats

Easy Science for Kids
http://easyscienceforkids.com

The Kid Should See This
http://thekidshouldseethis.com/post/how-do-plants-grow-in-space-science-friday

National Gardening Association
https://garden.org/learn/
Twitter: @NatlGardening,
Facebook: @Garden.Org, Instagram: @nationalgardeningassoc

INDEX